VIOLINJUDY'S

PANDA LULLABY

PIANO PRE-READING

SUPPLEMENTARY SONGS
FOR BEGINNING PIANO LEARNERS

 *Violin Judy's*

VERY FUN PIANO COLLECTION

Panda Lullaby by Judy Naillon

Copyright © 2023 ViolinJudy

www.violinjudy.com

ISBN: 978-1-960674-27-2

Violin Judy's
VERY FUN PIANO LIBRARY

A Pre-Reading Piano Lullaby is composed for beginning piano learners. Students using this book should be able to sit at the piano as many minutes as years of their age and recognize letters A-G and Numbers 1-5.

HOW TO USE QR CODES IN THIS BOOK:

SCAN ME

HOW TO SCAN A QR CODE WITH AN IPHONE OR IPAD:

BOTH IPHONES AND IPADS HAVE A QR SCANNER BUILT INTO THE CAMERA.

1. WITH A QR CODE NEARBY, OPEN THE CAMERA ON YOUR IPHONE OR IPAD.

2. POSITION THE CAMERA SO THE QR CODE IS IN FRAME. YOUR IPHONE OR IPAD SHOULD SCAN IT AUTOMATICALLY, WITHOUT ANY INPUT NEEDED FROM YOU. ONCE IT SCANS THE CODE, A NOTIFICATION WILL APPEAR AT THE TOP OF YOUR SCREEN WITH THE LINK TO THE QR CODE'S CONTENT. TAP THIS AND YOU'LL BE BROUGHT TO IT.

HOW TO SCAN A QR CODE WITH AN ANDROID PHONE OR TABLET:

ANDROID DEVICES HAVE THE QR CODE SCANNER BUILT INTO THE CAMERA. HOWEVER, YOU MIGHT NEED TO OPEN A SPECIAL APP TO USE IT.

1. WITH A QR CODE NEARBY, OPEN THE CAMERA ON YOUR ANDROID DEVICE.

2. POSITION THE CAMERA SO THE QR CODE IS IN FRAME. YOUR ANDROID SHOULD SCAN IT AUTOMATICALLY, BUT IF IT DOESN'T, PRESS AND HOLD YOUR FINGER ON IT YOU'LL BE GIVEN THE LINK THAT THE QR CODE LEADS TO AND A CHOICE TO OPEN IT, COPY THE URL, OR SHARE IT.

TABLE OF CONTENTS

NOTE TO TEACHERS/PRACTICE PARENT:

Any beginning piano student can start in this book on any keyboard or real piano. The pacing of this series is slower than any other method book you will find. This allows younger beginners time to really learn to read music as well as play a wide variety of songs. When you establish a firm foundation of technic, listening skills and songs students know and like to play, you'll have a pianist who learns to love music! Playing pieces that are traditional and familiar, yet presented in a fun, fresh way engages the learner.

We start with floating off-the-staff notes in this book. The pacing is graded in a manner that the note reading will not be overwhelming. Finger numbers are placed above or below the noteheads as an aide and phase out in higher level books as we focus on note reading building one note at a time with exercises and pieces using only the notes we have learned. The advantage of having a printed book to send home with learners helps everyone remember what and how to practice. Even young children are often able to practice these without help after the first few lessons or by watching the included instructional videos. You may use this book as a pre-cursor or in conjunction with common method books for young beginners.

In this book you will find many
tools to help learn piano including
FUN songs and worksheets!

Pieces in this book are fun to play in group lessons as well!
Students who have successfully completed this book can look forward to more skills to learn and fun pieces to master in *A Very Fun Piano Collection*
available on Amazon!

DO'S AND DON'TS FOR PIANO:

WASH YOUR HANDS BEFORE YOU PLAY OR PRACTICE PIANO.

SIT TALL WITH YOUR FEET ON THE GROUND. IF THEY DON'T REACH, FIND SOME EMPTY BOXES TO REST YOUR FEET ON.

HOLD YOUR ARMS OUT SO THEY TOUCH THE FALLBOARD OF THE PIANO. IF YOUR ARMS ARE NOT PARALLEL WITH THE GROUND, FIND SOMETHING TO SIT ON TO MAKE YOURSELF TALLER LIKE A BOOSTER SEAT, CUSHION OR PILLOW.

LOOK AT WHERE YOUR FINGERS GO BEFORE YOU START THE PIECE

COUNT YOURSELF OFF BEFORE YOU START:
"1-2-READY-PLAY" OR "1-2-READY-GO"

KEEP YOUR FINGERS GLUED TO THE KEYS UNTIL YOU'RE DONE PLAYING

PLAYING ON A KEYBOARD IS FINE, HOWEVER STARTING ON A KEYBOARD THAT MAKES LOUD AND SOFT SOUNDS (HAS TOUCH RESPONSE) WILL HELP YOU MAKE MORE BEAUTIFUL MUSIC

IF YOU'RE FEELING WIGGLY SEE IF YOU CAN BALANCE A STUFFED ANIMAL ON YOUR HEAD FOR 10 SECONDS!

CURVE YOUR FINGERS WHEN YOU PLAY PIANO LIKE YOU'RE CATCHING A BUBBLE!

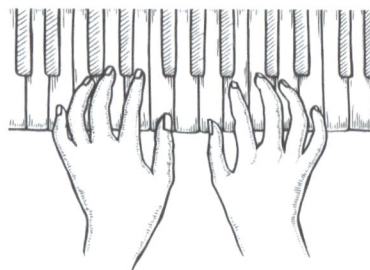

WHOLE NOTE	HALF NOTE	QUARTER NOTE	BASS CLEF
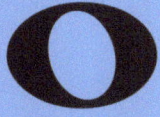			
"WHOLE NOTE HOLD IT" 4 BEATS	"HOLD ME" 2 BEATS	"QUARTER" 1 BEAT	USE YOUR LEFT HAND TO PLAY THESE NOTES

THREE BLACK KEYS	TWO BLACK KEYS	RIGHT HAND	TREBLE CLEF

USE YOUR "THREE YEARS OLD" FINGERS TO PLAY	USE YOUR "TWO YEARS OLD" FINGERS TO PLAY	USE THIS HAND TO PLAY UP STEM NOTES	USE YOUR RIGHT HAND TO PLAY THESE NOTES

LEFT HAND	HALF REST	QUARTER REST	REPEAT SIGN
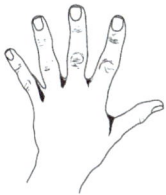			
USE THIS HAND TO PLAY DOWN STEM NOTES	HOLD 2 BEATS	HOLD 1 BEAT	PLAY AGAIN

DOUBLE BAR LINE	EIGHTH NOTES	BAR LINE	DOTTED HALF NOTE
THE END OF THE PIECE	RUNNING BUNNY= PLAY TWICE AS FAS AS QUARTER	CREATES MEASURES DON'T STOP!	"HOLD ME PLEASE" THREE BEATS

LULLABY PREFACE

SLEEPY TIME

Scan the QR code for a how-to video!

SCAN ME

4 4

3 3

2 2   2-

LULABIES ARE   VERY NICE,

4

3 3   2

BUT THEY MAKE ME SLEEPY,

3- 3-

3 3   4 4 4

2 2   3 3 3   4

MAYBE I'LL JUST   SHUT MY EYES

2 2 2

3 3 3   2- 2-

FOR A LITTLE DREAMY

CAN YOU LABEL THESE MISSING RIGHT HAND FINGERS WITH "BUNNY EARS" FINGER NUMBERS?

4

5

1

Fun Fact: Baby pandas are born pink!

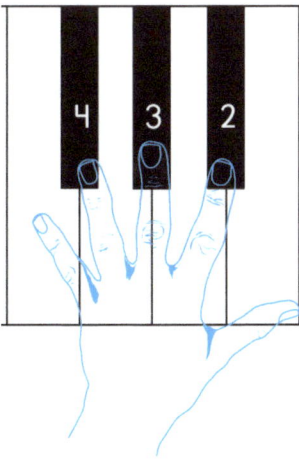

DREAM TEAM

SCAN ME

Need help?

𝄢 2 – | 2 – | 3 3   3 | 2 – – –
       4 4 | 4 – | 4 |

WE   ARE THE   DREAM   TEAM, HERE'S SWEET DREAMS FOR YOU!

𝄢 2 – | 2 – | 3 3 ² 3 | 4 – – –
       4 4 | 4 – |

WE   ONLY   WAKE   UP   FOR SOME FRESH BAMBOO!

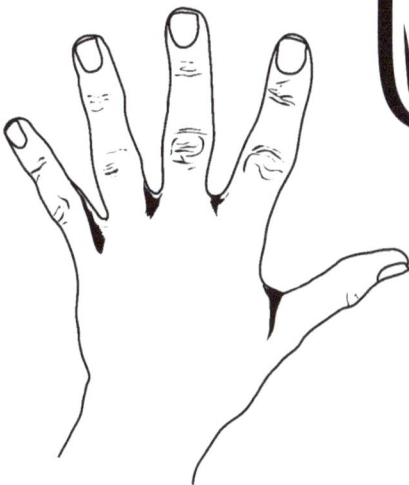

CAN YOU LABEL THESE LEFT HAND FINGERS WITH NUMBERS 1-5?

NAP SNACK

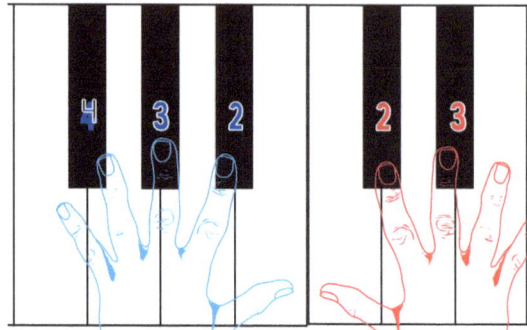

Watch a video here!

SCAN ME

𝄢 2 3 4 𝄽 | 4 3 2 𝄽 | 𝄞 3 - 3 - | 2 - 3 2 |

IT'S NAP TIME!   BUT I CAN'T   GO   TO   SLEEP 'CAUSE MY

𝄢 2 3 4 𝄽 | 4 3 2 𝄽 | 𝄞 3 - 2 2 | 𝄢 4 𝄽 4 𝄽 ‖

TUMMY GROWLS   MY LIPS SMACK!   I   NEED A   NAP   SNACK!

Can you label the missing fingers?

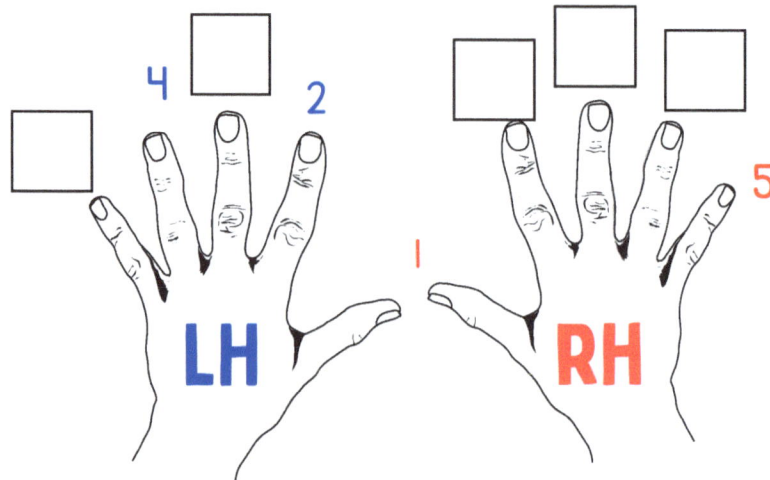

4   [ ]   2

[ ]

LH   1   RH

[ ] [ ] [ ]

5

STAR LIGHT, STAR BRIGHT

TRADITIONAL LULLABY
ARRANGED BY MRS. JUDY NAILLON

Watch out for a sneaky pinky!

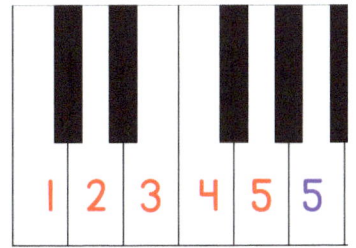

SCAN ME

START HERE

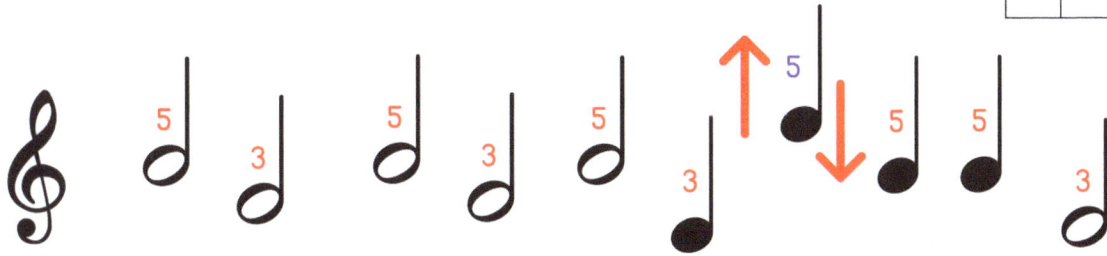

STAR LIGHT, STAR BRIGHT, FIRST STAR I   SEE TO-NIGHT

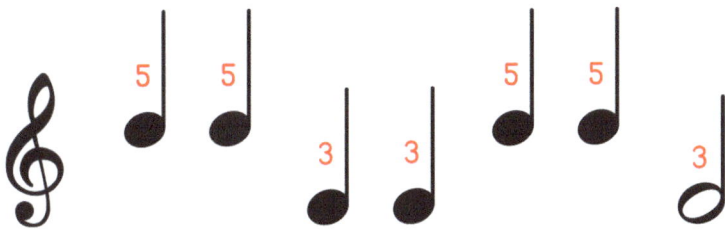

WISH I   MAY I   WISH I   MIGHT,

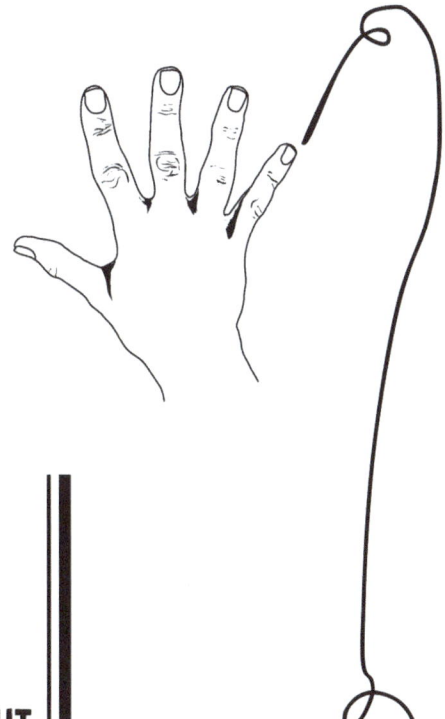

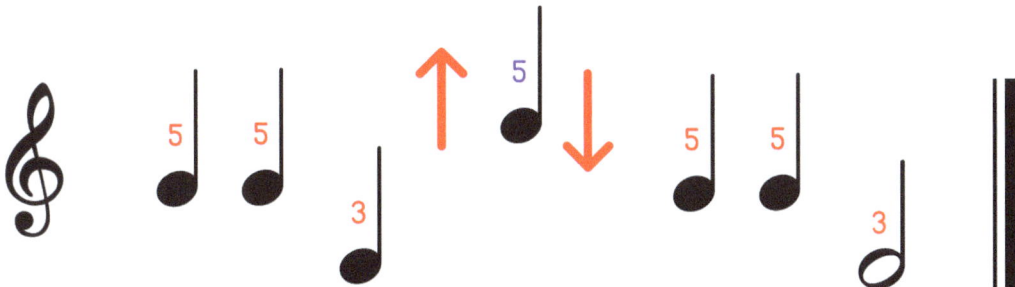

HAVE THE WISH   I   WISH   TO - NIGHT.

Draw a line from each panda to the finger on the hand that matches their heart!

Example:

SLEEP BABY SLEEP

12

Left hand doesn't get to play very much in this piece!

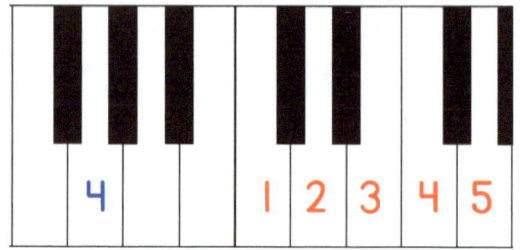

SCAN ME

TRADITIONAL LULLABY
ARRANGED BY MRS. JUDY NAILLON

START HERE

COLOR ALL THE D`S

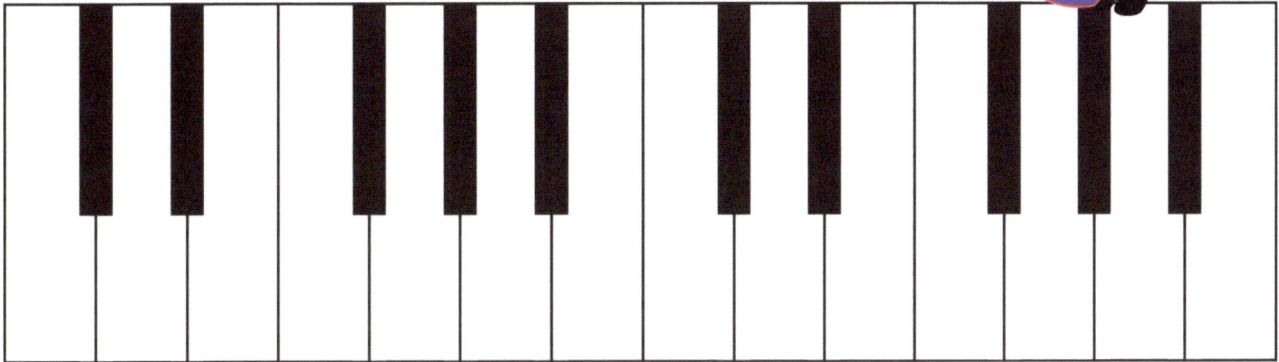

COLOR ALL THE G`S

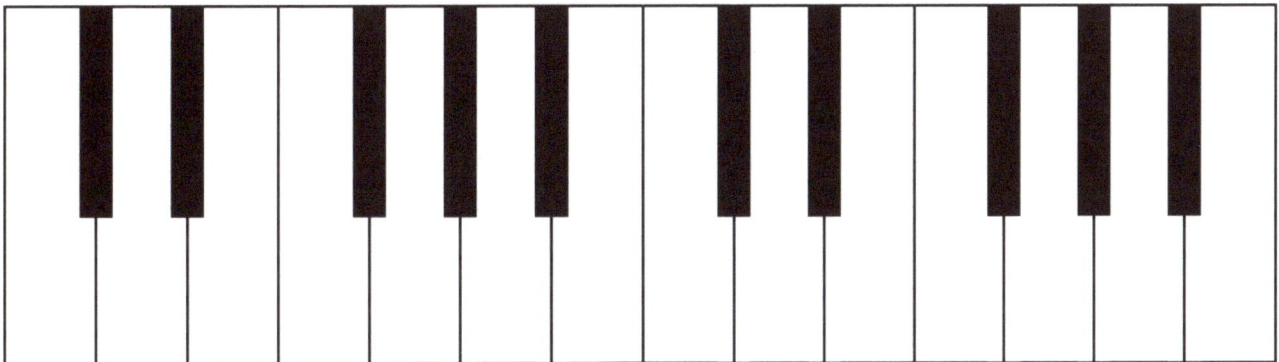

COLOR ALL THE A`S

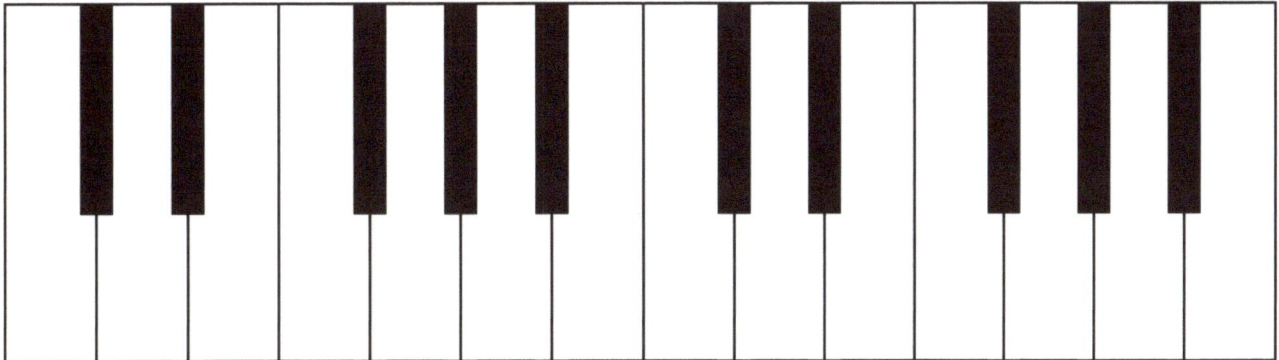

SCAN ME

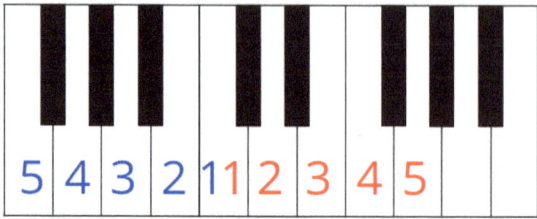

AMAZING GRACE

TRADITIONAL HYMN

LYRICS BY JOHN NEWTON

ARRANGED BY MRS. JUDY NAILLON

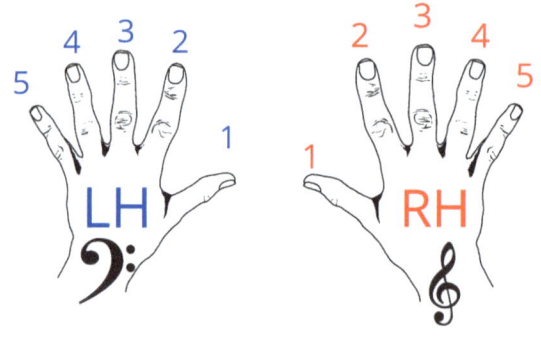

START HERE

FERMATA SIGN=HOLD
THIS NOTE LONGER

SCAN ME

COLOR ALL THE D'S

COLOR ALL THE C'S

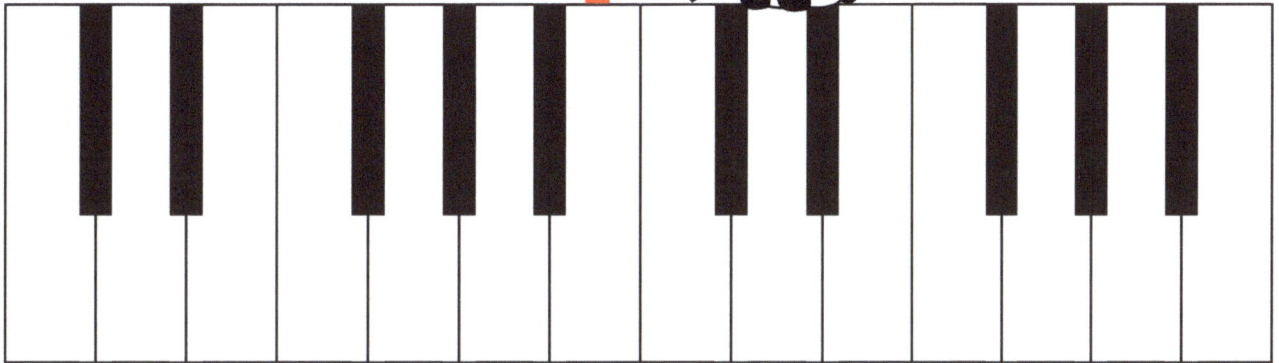

Learn the music alphabet
keyboard location in this video:

SCAN ME

COLOR ALL THE F'S

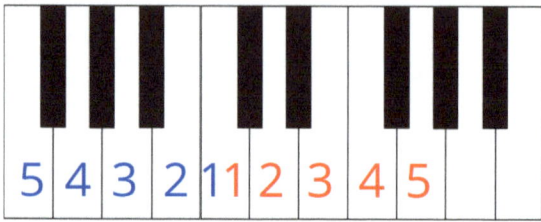

PRETTY LITTLE HORSES

TRADITIONAL LULLABY

ARRANGED BY MRS. JUDY NAILLON

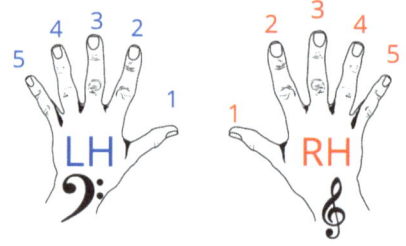

START HERE

REPEAT SIGN
PLAY THE FIRST LINE
AGAIN

SCAN ME

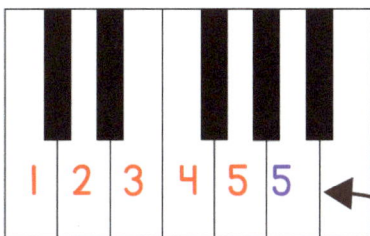

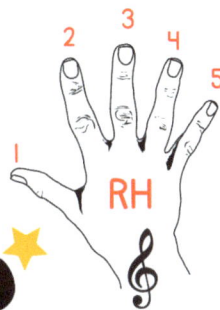

Draw a line from the "I'm three years old" fingers to the three black keys.
Pandas have five fingers on each hand AND a thumb.

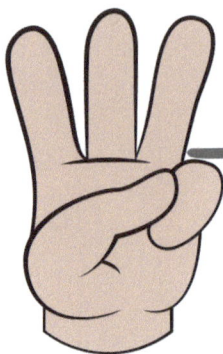

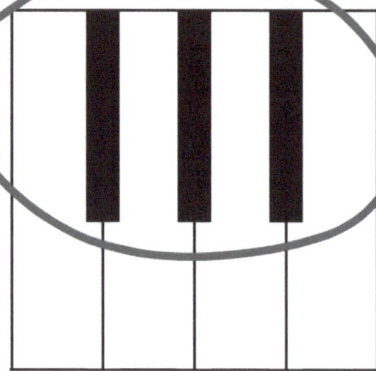

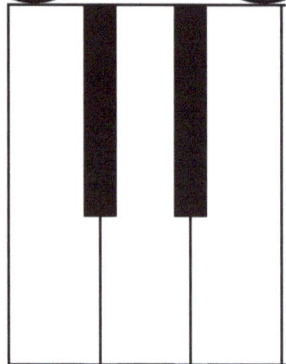

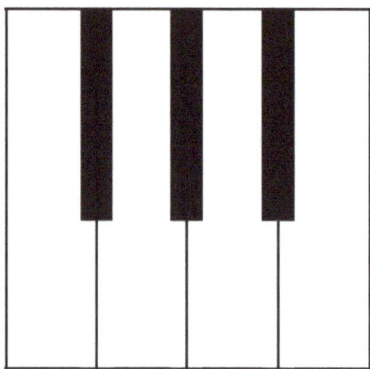

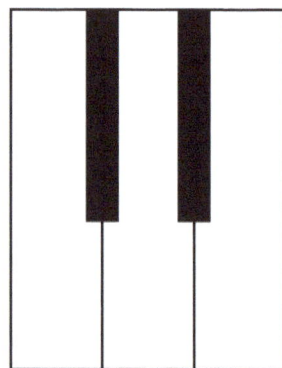

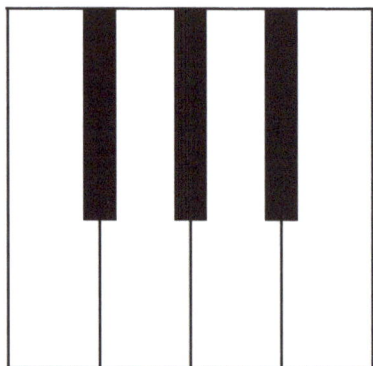

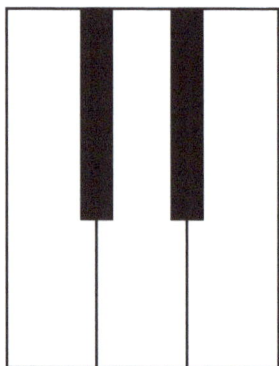

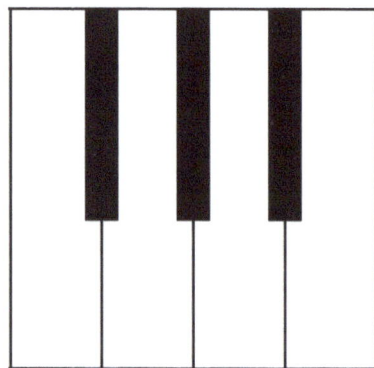

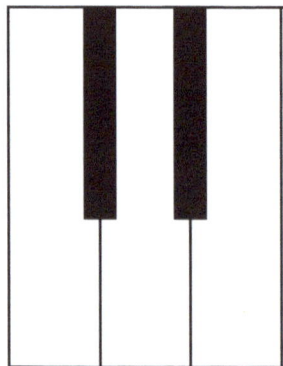

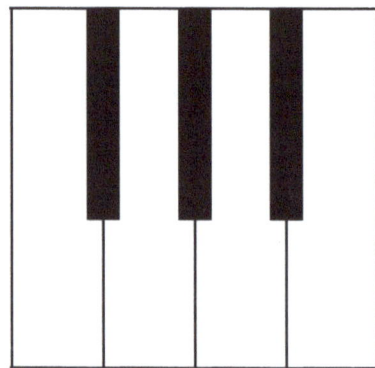

COLOR ALL THE E'S

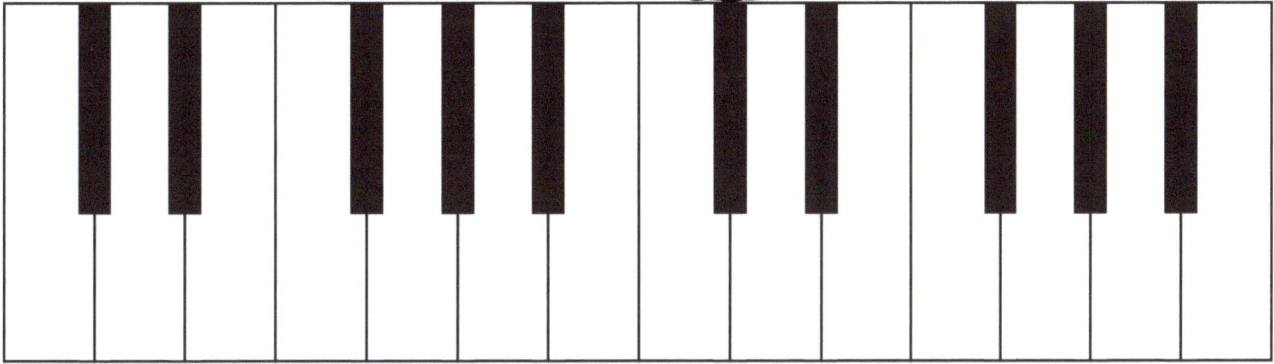

COLOR ALL THE B'S

SCAN ME

COLOR ALL THE C'S

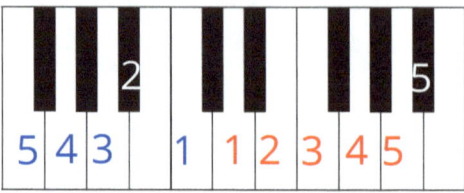

ROCK-A-BYE BABY

THIS PIECE HAS TWO BLACK KEYS!

BY: MOTHER GOOSE (TRADITIONAL)

ARRANGED BY MRS. JUDY NAILLON

START HERE

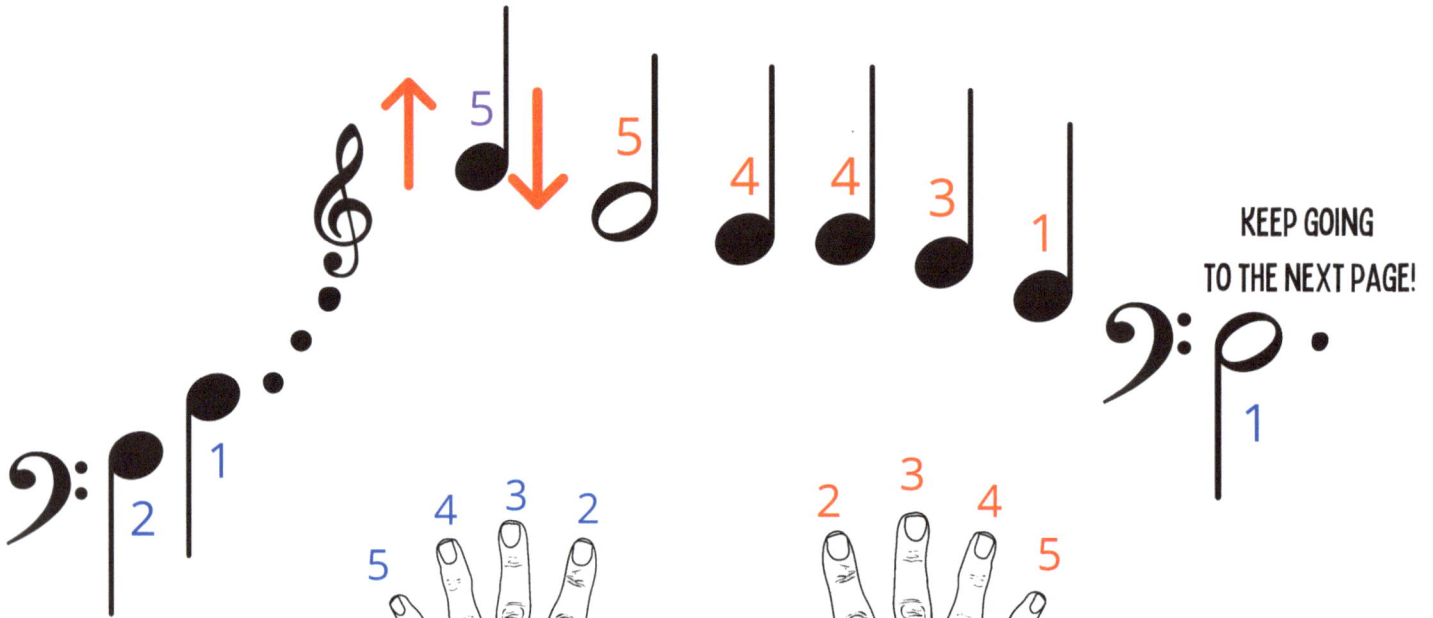

KEEP GOING TO THE NEXT PAGE!

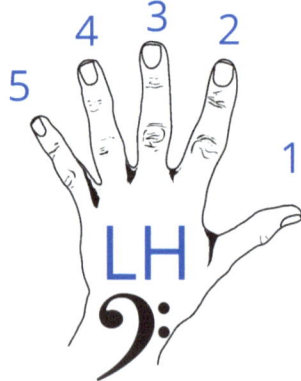

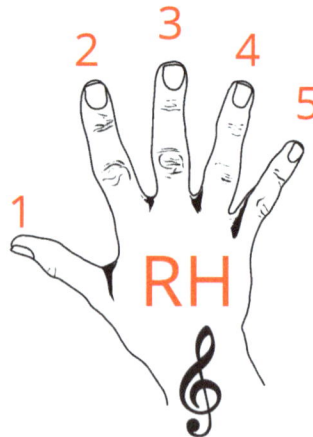

LH

RH

20

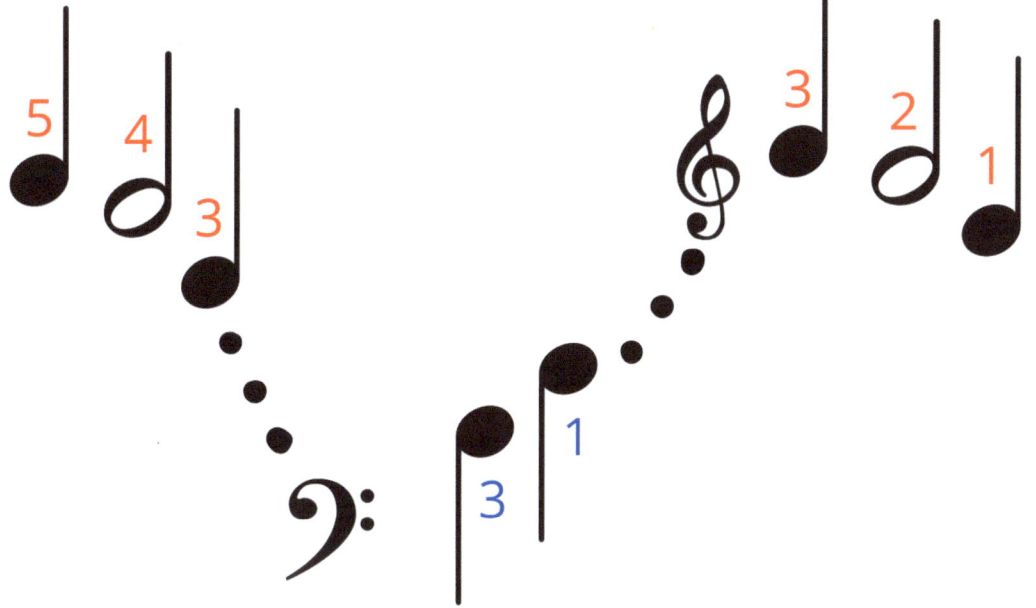

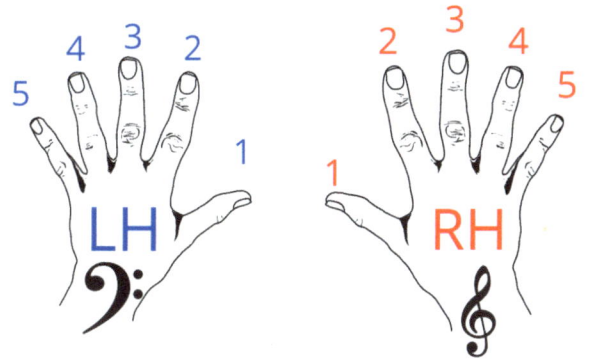

Label the hands right (R) or left (L)

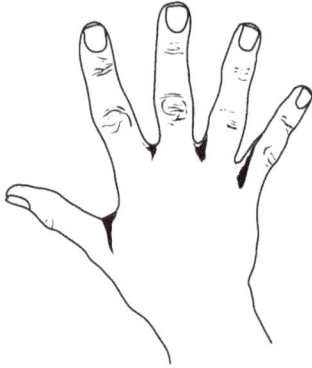

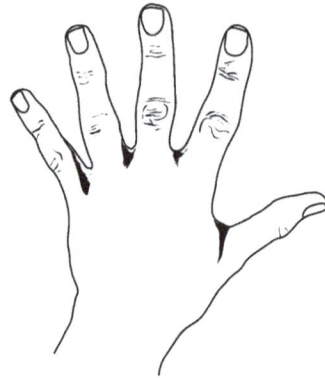

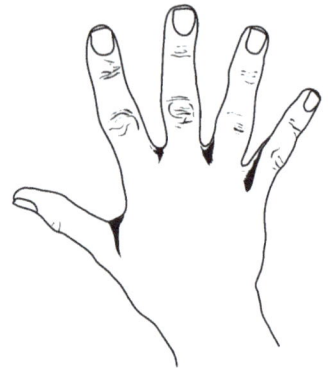

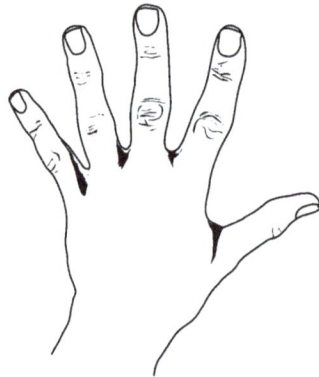

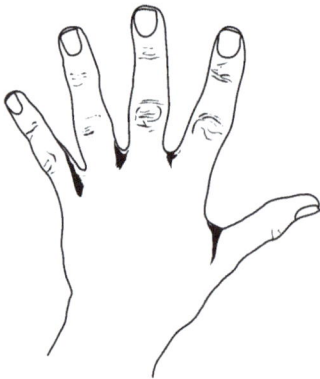

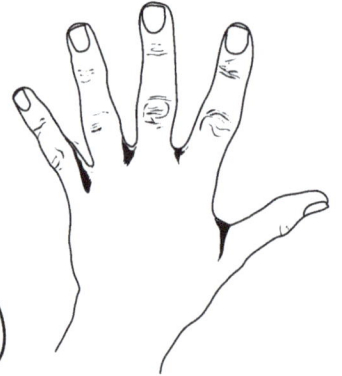

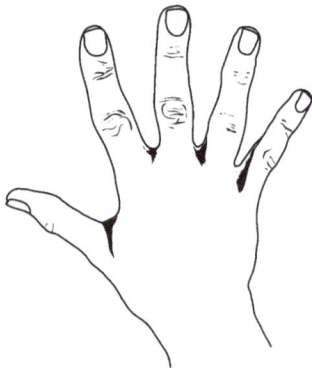

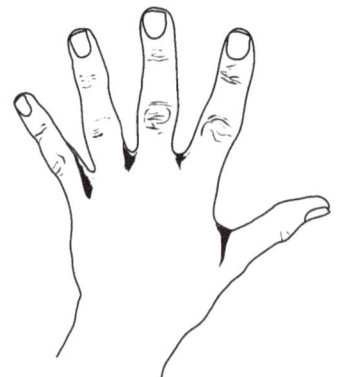

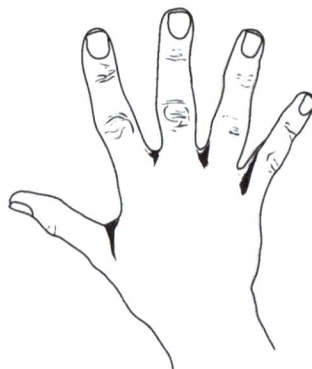

BEAMED 8TH NOTES

THIS IS A BEAM

THIS IS A BALANCE BEAM

WITH THE BEAM NOW
THESE ARE 8TH NOTES

IN MUSIC SOMETIMES NOTES HAVE A BEAM, THIS IS A LINE THAT CONNECTS THE STEMS TOGETHER. THIS IS SECRET CODE FOR FASTER NOTES! BUT HOW MUCH FASTER DO WE PLAY THESE NOTES? TWICE AS FAST AS A QUARTER NOTE. WHEN YOU SEE A QUARTER NOTE THINK "WALK" AND WHEN YOU SEE EITGHTH NOTES THINK "RUNNING"

TO HELP YOU REMEMBER TO PLAY BEAMED NOTES FASTER, WE HAVE REPLACED THE BEAMS WITH RUNNING BUNNIES IN THE NEXT PIECE- WHEN YOU SEE THE BUNNIES PLAY RUNNING-FASTER NOTES!

BRAHM`S LULLABY

BY: BRAHMS
ARRANGED BY
MRS. JUDY NAILLON

START HERE

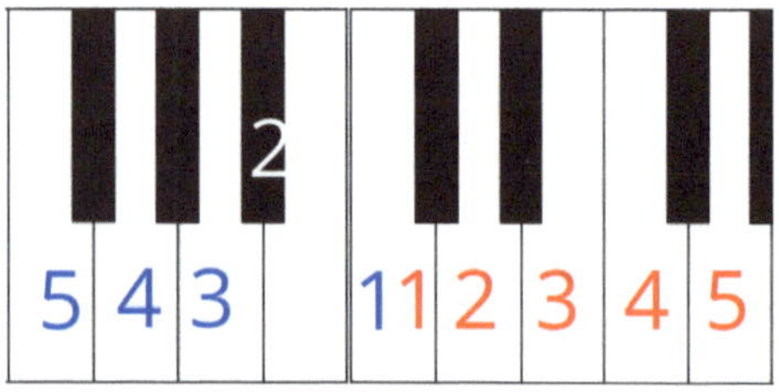

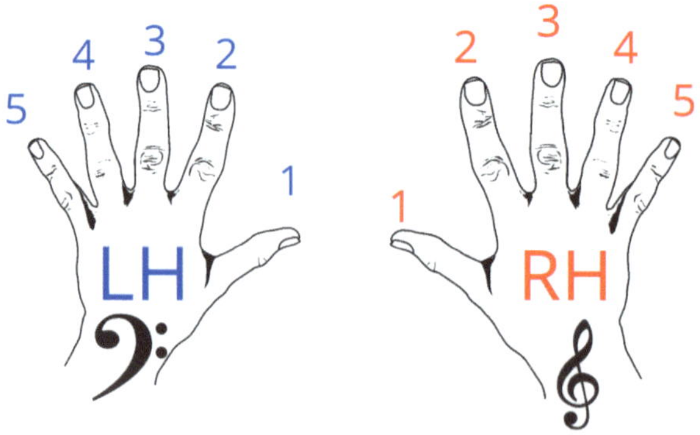

BRAHM`S LULLABY

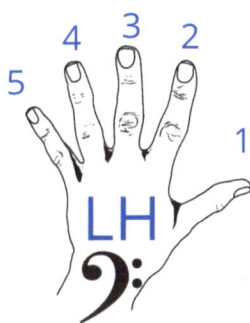

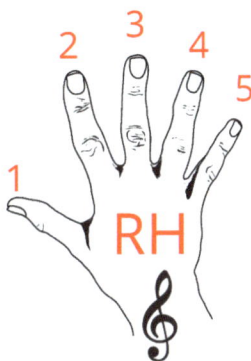

Draw a line from the "I'm two years old" fingers to the two black keys.

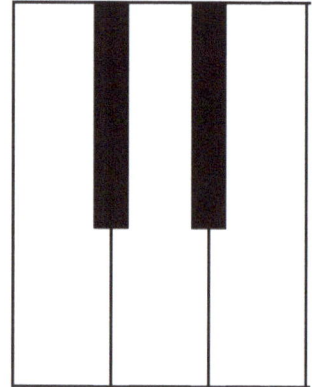

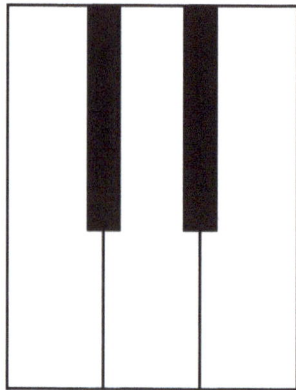

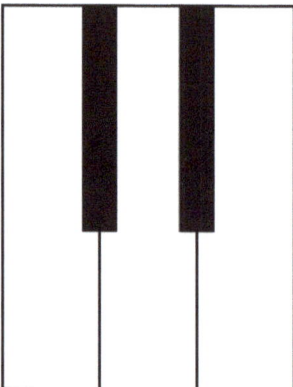

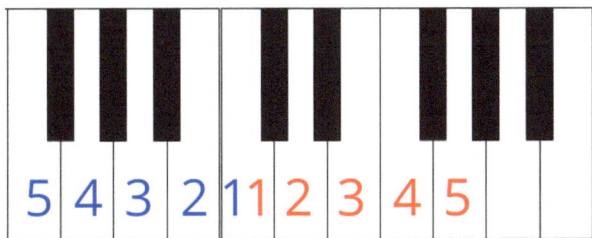

HUSH LITTLE BABY

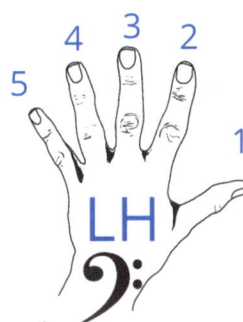

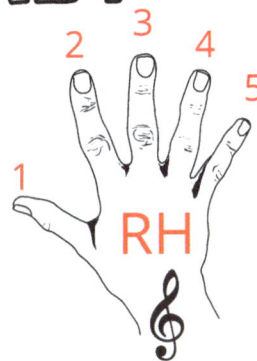

LH

RH

TRADITIONAL

ARRANGED BY MRS. JUDY NAILLON

START HERE

HUSH, LITTLE BABY DON`T SAY A WORD
PAPA`S GONNA BUY YOU A MOCKING BIRD

AND IF THAT MOCKING BIRD DON`T SING
PAPA`S GONNA BUY YOU A DIAMOND RING

AND IF THAT DIAMOND RING IS BRASS
PAPA`S GONNA BUY YOU A LOOKING GLASS

AND IF THAT LOOKING GLASS GETS BROKE
PAPA`S GONNA BUY YOU A BILLY GOAT

AND IF THAT BILLY GOAT DON`T PULL
PAPA`S GONNA BUY YOU A CART AND BULL

AND IF THAT CART AND BULL TURN OVER
PAPA`S GONNA BUY YOU A DOG CALLED ROVER

AND IF THAT DOG CALLED ROVER DON`T BARK
PAPA`S GONNA BUY YOU A HORSE AND CART

AND IF THAT HORSE AND CART TURN ROUND
YOU`LL STILL BE THE SWEETEST LITTLE BABE IN TOWN

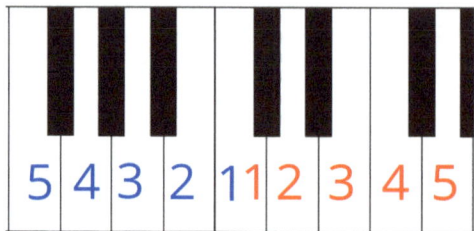

THE ASH GROVE

Pandas eat bamboo for up to 12 hours each day and 25 lbs. All that eating makes them sleepy!

SCAN ME

ALPHABET MAZE

Help the panda find his way to the bamboo through the music alphabet maze by connecting the notes in order:

START HERE:

END HERE!

A Q Z
X C
B J F
P U Y
C W
L D
D E B E
O K G
F A F
P G
Q R W Y
C X

BOOK LEVEL CHART FOR THE **VERY FUN PIANO LIBRARY**

PIANO GRADE	FUN PIANO LEVEL	MAIN CONCEPTS
PRE-READING FINGER LEARNING-EVERY FINGER LABELLED	A	USE FINGERS 1-5, BLACK KEY PIECES LEARN PIANO KEYS 4 BASIC RHYTHMS
PRE-READING DIRECTIONAL READING (LESS FINGER NUMBERS)	B	RUNNING BUNNY EIGHTH NOTES REINFORCE KEY NAMES
PRE-READING NOTE LETTERS IN NOTE HEADS	C	BEGIN TO LEARN NOTE NAMES AND KEYBOARD LOCATION
NOTE READING	D	ONLY LANDMARK NOTES WITH LETTERS AND FINGERS LABELLED
NOTE READING	E	DECODE WHERE HANDS GO ON THE PIANO KEYBOARD

Violin Judy

Mrs. Judy Naillon, or "ViolinJudy" is a dedicated and enthusiastic independent piano and violin teacher, composer, and professional violinist. Her work consists of her large private music studio, as well as playing with her string quartet and Local Professional Orchestra. She served as a church musician for over 20 years and is active in leadership in the musicians' union. She loves coming up with creative ideas to help both students and teachers be successful and blogs about it all at www.ViolinJudy.com and for Alfred's Music Publishers. When she is not writing new books she loves spending time with her family and little dog Pom.

CERTIFICATE

OF ACHIEVEMENT

This awarded to :

----

for the achievement of the completion of:

Teacher

Date